U·P·S·T·A·T·E

Living Spaces with Space to Live

Photographs by Sarah Elliott

Lisa Przystup

U·P·S·T·A·T·E

Living Spaces with Space to Live

THE MONACELLI PRESS

I've always had a preoccupation with homes. First and foremost, with the poetry that the very idea of home offers: a place that you can always return to, a place that takes you back to who you are at your very core. With the heartbreak of home: losing your first, which in a way means losing part of your childhood. And with growing up and creating a new home, for yourself, maybe for yourself and a partner, and then maybe even for a family.

   Living in New York City for a decade, I developed an infatuation with the idea that each person's small apartment contained multitudes. I loved that you can walk up to an unremarkable building, step inside a dimly lit hallway that never quite smells right, climb all those tedious stairs, knock on a door, and enter a secret jewel box, a personal hideaway. In a city where we are constantly brushing up against other people, these diminutive apartments serve as our havens of a sort—their size only concentrating their impact—layers on layers, tchotchkes upon tchotchkes.

This leads me to my second obsession re: homes: the mechanics of making one. The act of nesting. Collecting, curating, arranging—every move purposeful and thoughtful and entirely unique to each person—a fingerprint. I've always loved this—creating a world designed to bring pleasure and warmth and comfort is infinitely appealing and endlessly gratifying.

My husband and I spent eight years happily orbiting the universe of our Greenpoint railroad apartment, but then a strange (yet wholly expected) thing started to happen. With each clamorous trash pickup outside our window and every pointless 311 call I made to complain about the same minivan playing music at 3 a.m., the walls of our apartment began closing in and, like many before us, we looked to upstate New York for room.

A home upstate can mean just that: ROOM. Room to breathe, room to spread out, and at its most literal, rooms (as in many)—acres of bedrooms, ambitious backyards, winding banistered staircases that lead to second and third floors. The transition from a postage stamp of an apartment to a whole house was exhilarating and jarring all at once; the possibilities felt endless, which also felt overwhelming. When you live in a tiny apartment, the limited space dictates where things go: there was only one place our dresser could fit and no room for a couch and the kitchen table had to live in the only space it could. These constraints offered a kind of freedom—the freedom found in not having to make a choice, in being able to focus on the smaller details of creating a home. The vastness of an honest-to-goodness house makes it hard to know where to begin. But once you do, it's thrilling.

All the ideas I had been filing away in the storage unit of my brain finally had a purpose. We were scrappy when it came to finding furniture and made it a point to search Craigslist and eBay, and scrounge around local yard sales and antique stores for pieces to bring home. In the end, the identity of our home up here is wrapped up in what it means to us: Escape. Freedom. A deep breath. A place to host family and friends. This simple fact means that it and everything it houses enjoys the generous gaze of rose-colored glasses. Every piece, every room feels meaningful—to me, that's what makes living upstate unique.

Each upstate home that Sarah Elliott and I captured belongs so thoroughly, so specifically to the people who live in them. Every house had a design detail, an arrangement, a piece of furniture, or paint color that I wanted to recreate in my own home. I found myself coveting, and then I came to a very trite but true realization: each home is special for the same reason that every person is. I can't be any of the homeowners because, well, I'm not, and our home is exactly as it's supposed to be for us. That's what makes it exceptional. That's what makes it ours.

In the same way that Andrea Gentl's kitchen witch's apothecary is uniquely hers, or that Don Howell and Ray Camano's beautifully patinaed home is theirs, or that Cary Leibowitz and Simon Lince's rainbow-streamer sitting room is theirs. The feeling of a home is tied directly to the people who live in it: their tastes, their life stories, their personalities. It is much more (and more significant) than interior decoration or designer furniture, though those can be part of it too. Every homeowner I visited with had some small tip. Don Howell shared his limewash recipe, Mimi Madigan taught me how to get moss to grow on stone walls and walkways (combine beer, sugar, and some existing moss in a blender, and apply to stone with a paintbrush), and Sara and Sohail Zandi can tell you all about removing the yellow from pine floors (sanding, lots and lots of sanding). And each also had a string of anecdotes, such as rescuing rose bushes with silver spoons, or having inquisitive squirrels pop their heads out of bedroom walls. The list goes on.

I found very quickly that each small town north of the city has its own special community—a group of people who had followed the same call we did to carve out their own personal slice of land and sky and peace and quiet. I also found that people's homes up here are just as wonderfully surprising as those city apartments. For some, they're a weekend retreat. Others have made the leap from the city to upstate and have created full-time lives, businesses, worlds. And even some had the good sense to have been born and raised here—native or lifelong upstaters, who know what it is to grow up with what for some of us is a beautiful novelty or an exception to the rule. They know more about what it means to live upstate than we newbies ever will.

One day we will all leave our houses and someone else will fill them with their touch, their memories, their truths. This to me is the enduring magic of a home and something I sought to share about the spaces in this book and the people who made them what they are.

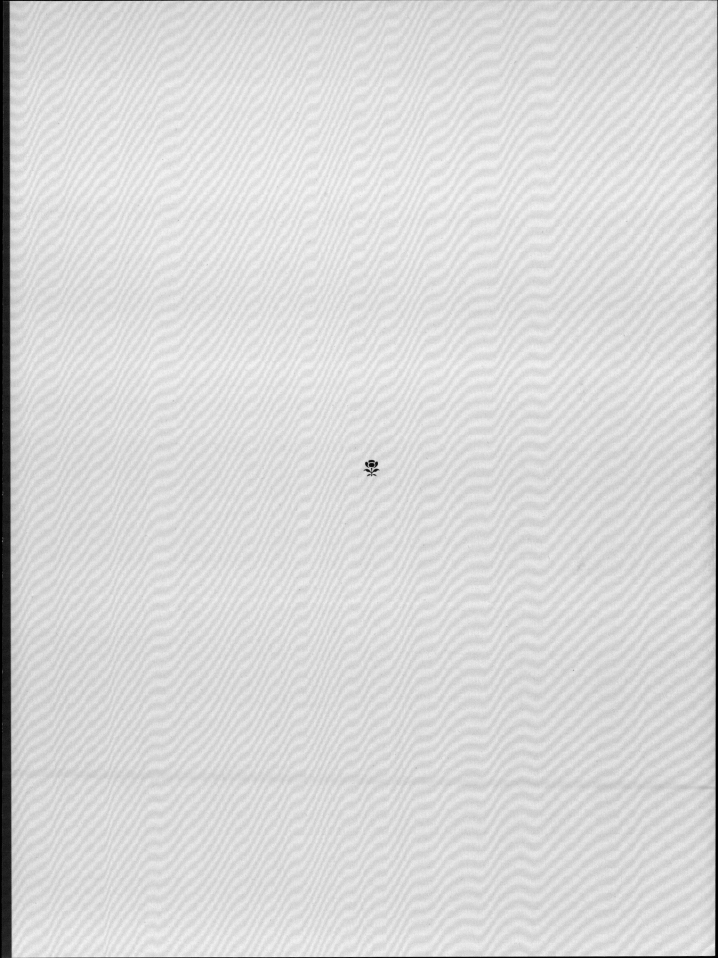

Jonathon and I had looked at at least fifteen terrible (well, maybe not terrible, but disappointing) houses upstate before we found the one we ended up buying, in Delhi. There was no "aha" moment when we saw it. It was nice. We liked it. It sat at the top of a very long, precipitous, unplowable driveway (we didn't know it yet, but several friends would manage to slide their cars into the sneaky ditches that run alongside, and we'd dig them out). It had a staircase with a tight curve of fanned steps at the base that spoke to me, but, then again, almost any staircase speaks to me, especially one that isn't lit by a harsh fluorescent light leading to an overpriced apartment in an overpriced city. The house upstate came with five acres, which felt like a lot, but then I had no real understanding of what an acre was (and really still don't). I just know that it means land and possibility.

DELHI

1893

   Our home is wrapped in strips of dented aluminum siding; hornets float in and out every August and September. The eaves are peeling, and the window and door frames need to be replaced. It's been a few years since we bought it and our to-do list reads

predictably long and boring, like any homeowner's. But the magic of the house exists in equal measure. Here is what makes it its most spellbinding, in no particular order: 1. The sun reflecting off snow and flooding the house with fantastic, bright, otherworldly light. 2. The sound and spectacle of the crickets and grasshoppers and lightning bugs 3. It is ours.

The stages of our home's evolution were dictated by financial and creative wherewithal. The first stage involved a lot of white paint (floors, walls, everything). The second addressed furniture placement. We are currently in the third stage, which primarily involves second- and third-guessing everything we established in the second stage.

Unlike many of the homes in this book, ours hasn't really been informed by what we do for a living (he's a musician, I'm a writer) or how we met (I was a waitress, he was a regular). Instead its identity comes from the things and people we love: the friends and family we've hosted have shaped the house in intangible ways that can't be photographed, which to me only proves their importance. And as far as physical evidence of our personalized marks goes, there are the objects pilfered from the yard or pocketed on upstate walks or discovered on road trips (see Exhibit A: a tumbleweed found on the side of the highway in Arizona that enjoyed a cross-country ride on my lap). There are rounded, smooth rocks picked up at beaches and so many shells that they're basically redundant. There is a baby grand piano that belonged to Jonathon's mother and to her mother before and so on and so forth until we're able to say, with reverence and pride, that it's over one hundred years old.

Sometime in between mowing the lawn and building a cage for our blueberry bushes or splitting wood or sowing seeds, Jonathon will sit down to play, always for too short a time. And if you haven't had the pleasure of hearing the sounds of a piano fill your home, then please, by all means, come over. Slide off our driveway. We'll dig you out.

UPSTATE

Handmade details and weekend projects fill the house. In the kitchen, a mounted brass sheet is an unconventional but beautifully patinaed backsplash. Curtains made from a linen hand towel filter sunlight that streams into the breakfast area.

I'm a compulsive collector of any bits and pieces from nature that I can get my hands on. The curio cabinet is my place to corral them all.

Jonathon's childhood turned-wood bed was rediscovered in a storage space above his uncle's garage. It now lives in a guest bedroom.

UPSTATE

Claire Benoist was at a wine tasting in Long Island when a real estate ad popped up on her phone. She idly clicked on it, and a listing for an 1892 iron foundry–turned-residence flashed onto her screen. "I couldn't wrap my head around it! Here was this huge loft-like space that I had dreamt of having in the city all through my twenties," she says. She showed it to her husband, Derek Kilner, who laughed. "The whole time I was growing up, my parents would buy these weird old places," says Claire. Her research scientist parents—her father, French; her mother, American—met at a lab in Strasbourg, had Claire in Palo Alto, and then returned to France, where they lived until Claire was sixteen and the family relocated one last time, to Boston.

Finding and renovating a shuttered iron foundry/former artist commune had the reassuring feeling of history repeating itself for Claire. When she was a baby, her parents bought an eighteenth-century traditional Alsatian half-timbered house in a small town outside of Strasbourg and their first winter there the family lived with plastic sheeting covering the holes where the old windows had been. Then, when Claire was eleven, her parents worked with an architect to convert former bank offices in Strasbourg into an

SOMERS

1892

apartment, tearing down the tiny cubicles and creating an open living space. At their front entry was a triple-reinforced vault door. But while Claire is, in her words, "reckless and emotional," Derek is pragmatic. As it turns out, this is the ideal combination when embarking on an ambitious renovation of a historical industrial building.

When the couple first saw the space, the kitchen, living room, and dining room were crowded together in the basement, and the bedroom occupied what is now their kitchen on the second floor. They whitewashed the basement and poured white concrete floors, repurposing it as a space for guests. Then they moved the kitchen upstairs, beneath the overhang of a lofted bedroom that overlooks most of the second floor ("My grandparents had a little lofted space at their home in Paris just like this one and it reminds me of my childhood," says Claire). The view from there is of a scene shaped by Claire's keen eye—honed through her career as a beauty and still-life photographer. Throughout the home modern pieces mingle effortlessly with her parents' antiques.

"It's a very old house with a modern renovation and the furniture mirrors that," she says. One piece, a formidable wood slab table—an early purchase made by Claire's parents for their home in Strasbourg—anchors the kitchen with a weighty familiarity. "I have a picture of this table from my fifth birthday party with all my friends sitting around it and a big cake in the middle," says Claire. Her parents had the table—along with a Seltz bedroom set and a round Pierre Chapo dining table that can be found softening the corner of Claire and Derek's bedroom—brought over from France when they moved to Boston.

"It was so nice to have something real to start with," Claire says of her parents' pieces. "We didn't have plans for this,"—a gut renovation of an old foundry—"but when I saw the space I realized that *this* could be the plan. When I walked in and saw the possibilities, I felt like I could breathe."

A Malm fireplace standing center stage in the living room highlights the soaring ceiling with its graceful lines and makes for a snug focal point in winter.

PALO ALTO

UPSTATE

A large seating cushion at the front entrance can be tucked away in a hidden compartment when not in use. A Panton chair reframes an antique table that belonged to Claire's great-grandmother.

A vintage Seltz bedroom set and a Pierre Chapo table that belonged
to Claire's parents find a home in the bedroom.

Christiana Mavromatis and Scott Arnold learned that the roots of the tree standing next to their 1890s-era Tannersville home were holding so much water that the house was rotting from underneath, which meant that the couple had a tough decision. "Cut down a beautiful mature tree or lose up to twenty feet of the library," says Christiana. "I didn't want to do either." The tree stayed. Afterward, the couple learned that cutting the library back had inadvertently restored the room to its original dimensions—a big check in their plus column. "Reverting to the original design of the house was 100 percent our North Star, so when we were on the fence or didn't know how to make a decision, it was, Okay, what was the original intention or design or purpose and how can we reflect that?"

The exposed wood beams in the dining room are a part of that reflection. Original to the house, they were covered in a milky gray pickling finish. It took Scott four months of sanding—perched on the top of a ladder and reaching over his head—to uncover the 120-year-old wood underneath. "It's my Sistine Chapel," he laughs.

TANNERSVILLE

c. 1895

Scott and Christiana had already successfully pulled off a gut renovation of their Park Slope home, but a seven-bedroom, seven thousand-square-foot undertaking was another thing altogether. They wanted to do everything they could to honor the integrity of the Tannersville house, which is where Tara Mangini and Percy Bright of Jersey Ice Cream Co. came in. The design team had amassed a cult following thanks in part to their unique design approach: they live in (or near) each home they work on and outfit it from top to bottom, redesigning, renovating, furnishing, and styling in one fell swoop. "I remember Tara was in the ballroom"—added after the sprawling three-floor former inn was converted to a private home in the 1950s—and she said, 'We don't have to change a thing!' and I was like, 'Right? That's obviously not true, but I know what you mean!'" laughs Christiana.

When the renovations were done, Scott and Christiana had a fully formed home, to which the couple added pieces of sentimental value. A gilded treasure chest that sits on the landing—"Perfect for the spirit of the house: a totally impractical, ridiculous, whimsical, beautiful, magnificent thing"—was a gift from Christiana's parents. "As a kid growing up in London my parents would go antiquing and drag me and my brother along. I was about eight or nine, we were at one of their favorite shops and my brother and I were playing hide-and-seek when I saw this gold treasure chest. I was transfixed," says Christiana. A rug in the yellow bedroom is another artifact from Christiana's childhood, bought at Harrods in the 1980s. "I grew up lying on that rug, tracing the patterns with my fingers," she says.

While Percy and Tara largely shaped the interior of the house, Scott and Christiana have formed its spirit with an abiding sense of purpose and commitment. "We said to each other, instead of trying to tell our kids over and over again about what they could or should do in life, let's show them. They can watch us do this and they'll be a part of this experience, and that idea was the glue that held this bad reasoning together," laughs Scott. "When we turned forty together we said, 'Let's look back when we turn fifty and let's talk about how much we did.'"

A handsome framed tapestry—a fortuitous flea-market find—anchors
a rustic but refined sitting area.

Beneath the house's original 120-year-old wood beams, which were patiently refinished by Scott over four months—he calls the project his Sistine Chapel—a long, welcoming table draws family and guests to the dining room.

Vintage hairbrushes and a hand mirror discovered in the home are
a beautiful collection and an ode to days past. "When we bought the
house, they were sitting out on vanities, tucked into drawers, resting in
front of mirrors, waiting to be picked up and used," says Christiana.

The front door of Andrea Gentl and Martin Hyers's Hamden home opens directly into their kitchen, so that coming in for a dinner party in late May feels almost like walking out of an apartment building onto a New York City sidewalk: that electric sensation of being enveloped by a buzz of happy, frenetic energy. Andrea, warm and steady, mixes cocktails in a glass pitcher; Marty, tall and gregarious, chats with guests, each of them tackling some food prep, a collective effort that culminates in a candlelit dinner at the couple's long dining table.

HAMDEN

c. 1890
& 1999

Andrea and Marty are thoroughly comfortable in a room full of people, a situation in which they find themselves often, and all over the world. As photographers, they are prolific travelers—Sweden, Peru, Burma, Nepal, Italy, Istanbul, Mexico, Ireland—and their photographs, saturated tableaux of far-flung meals in medias res and perceptive portraits of local faces, reveal their affection for people and for food. On a kitchen shelf, glass canisters filled with a miscellany of ingredients vie for limited real estate. "Andrea is an herb, Chaga, bean, root, and flour

hoarder," says Marty. "Each jar contains something that, for us, is a little chapter of our life together. One jar has a leafy incense that we brought back from Burma. One has ground pine we brought from India. One has Chaga that we got from a forager friend." Andrea laughs, "It's my witchy apothecary."

When the couple bought their property twenty-one years ago, it came with a small house, circa 1880. The house had no electricity, no indoor bathroom, and in the walls were beehives loaded with honey. It was beyond rehabilitation. So they tore it down and started from the ground up. The new house went up in the spring: same spot, same size, same orientation as the original. "We collected house parts over the winter: paneling from a courthouse, light switch covers from a yard sale, stairs from a telegraph house," says Marty. "The floors came out of a barn in Vermont and they smelled like cow pee," adds Andrea.

The house is a case study in how to build something new that truly feels old, as if it had "lived many lives," the couple says. They hired a local woodworker to make the windows following 1930s-era plans, and sourced wavy restoration glass for their panes. Even the arrangement of the house's floorboards is deliberately idiosyncratic, starting left from the door, then jogging right halfway in.

Behind all this attention to detail is a sort of wild romance that seems fundamental to their home, work, and lives. Case in point: the rose bushes out front that Marty rescued from a neighbor's down the road. "I dug them up with a silver serving spoon on a hot August day," he says. "I found out later that two sisters from England brought them over on a ship and planted them there 130 years ago."

Or the cabinet in the upstairs hallway that houses "anything that wants to be there," says Marty. "If I dug up an artifact from the yard, I would know instantly where it wanted to go. There are letters from the walls of the original house, my daughter's hair, a Civil War cutlass from my great-grandfather, there are playing cards from abandoned houses, birds' nests, cigar boxes that held someone's photographs, there are mouse bones and crystals, there are drawings and maps." He adds, "Our house is a three-dimensional scrapbook of our lives together. Each thing in it represents a moment in our life and, in a way, each object was a living participant in finding its way to us."

UPSTATE

"It started with a simple group of candlesticks," Marty says of the collection on the fireplace mantel. "And now it's a Jenga stack of fragile things held together by friction and balance."

"The glass jars in the kitchen are full of things that comprise my wild pantry," says Andrea. "I cook with all that stuff. I'm constantly collecting things for the upstate pantry and drying or pickling them."

UPSTATE

UPSTATE

The shelves in Andrea and Marty's bedroom are stacked with recipe, photography, and art books. The mission dresser was the first piece of furniture the couple purchased together.

Simon Lince and Cary Leibowitz's home exudes a madcap whimsy and it's easy to get swept up in their aesthetic, a very palatable flavor of Kool-Aid. In a sitting room, festoons of rainbow streamers hang from the ceiling, leftover holiday trimmings strung up by Simon. "They started drooping down to where they were brushing your head," he says. "I thought about taking them down, but I strung a streamer across the middle instead." In their bedroom, a banner of multicolored cut-out letters wishes them HAPPY NEW YEAR 2019. Made by Simon's niece and nephew years ago, Simon just updates the last number to reflect the current year.

Simon and Cary met nineteen years ago through the artist Katharine Umsted, whose piece *Endless Column* is the focal point of their upstairs guest room. "She described us to each other and we were both like, 'Why would you think we'd be interested in each other?'" says Simon. "Then a year later we actually met at her gallery and we were like, 'Oh this is *him*? He's nothing like what you said.' We never looked back." In addition to matching suits (of the psychedelic floral and campy bark cloth variety) the couple shares a wicked sense of humor that permeates the house. Drinking glasses designed by Cary are emblazoned with cheeky phrases ("Abraham Lincoln's

GHENT

1795
& 2009

Friend Sleeps Over," "George Washington Redecorates Mount Vernon," and "Better Not Say Anything Bad About Liza") and a collection of mugs features the entire House of Windsor. Then there are the giant corn-on-the-cob side tables. And the technicolor mushroom table-and-chair set, a Price Chopper find. The plastic lilac garland that wraps its way up the stairs— "I probably only paid a dollar for it," says Cary—is a beautiful bit of kitsch softening the collection of antique Mount Vernon group photos that crowd the walls.

Plastic garland notwithstanding, Simon's penchant for gardening is clear outside—where he's sweet-talked a thriving garden into existence—and in—where he arranges freshly cut blooms in a pair of 1960s-era flower stands that Cary found at auction. "Everywhere I've lived, I've had a garden: London, New York, Toronto, Dusseldorf . . . " he says.

Cary even commissioned custom wallpaper crisscrossed with forsythia, one of Simon's favorite flowers, for the master bedroom.

The house itself is a wonderful mishmash of old and new: the original section dates to 1795, and an addition, by architects Robert Venturi (with whom Simon shares a birthday) and Denise Scott Brown, to 2009. "We realized that we needed a bigger room. . . . There were no larger walls for hanging art," says Cary as he stands up and flips a switch. On the wall, a painting, by Jonathan Borofsky, begins to spin.

Cary and Simon's house is decorated with a mash-up of furniture in different styles, including, overleaf, postmodern treasures such as a Michele De Lucchi Memphis chair. The yellow sofa was won at a charity auction held by Oprah.

Statuettes of American presidents (found at two antique shops in
Hudson) perch on pedestals in the bathroom. A collection of group
portraits taken at Mount Vernon—and *George Washington* by Alex
Katz—lines the stairway.

The zigzag floors in the addition are industrial linoleum tiles laid in what Cary describes as a "Renaissance pattern." A plexiglass fireplace designed by Robert Venturi (and cheekily emblazoned with the faces of Venturi and Denise Scott Brown) provides a backdrop to the whimsical dining furniture by the architects.

UPSTATE

Piles of books and floral wallpaper make the guest bedroom
a cheerful retreat. Installed in the room is Katharine Umsted's
Endless Column.

Pulling up to Don Howell and Ray Camano's house
in Accord, the first thing you notice is its quiet sort
of wildness. There's a smattering of moss on the roof
and the (unused) front door opens out to an encroach-
ing sea of feral ferns. Standing on the stone patio
feels like being on the stage of an impressive theater,
a wide panorama of unbridled growth where rows and
rows of seats should be.

ACCORD

c. 1830

    "The house is a little Grey Gardens—we don't like
to admit it, but it is," laughs Ray, recounting finding
himself face-to-face with a squirrel that had popped
its head out of their bedroom wall.

    In the late 1990s, when the couple found the 1830s
house after a six-month search that started in Colum-
bia County and ended in Ulster, it had been sitting
abandoned for forty years. They spotted it online in
a Poughkeepsie newspaper ad. "This was unheard of
because it was 1999. There was this picture of a place
that I could tell was a very simple Greek Revival, with
a waterfall and twenty acres—completely untouched,"
says Don. "The real estate agent was really smart
because he took us on a tour of the property first and

after I saw it I said, 'I don't care what it takes to fix that house, this property is amazing!'" adds Ray.

When Don and Ray first visited, a large section of floorboards and areas of the ceiling were missing; the previous owner had replaced the roof in order to keep the house from further deterioration and that was about it. The couple started making it livable from the outside, replacing roughly a quarter of the exterior and rubbing the new wood with mud from the nearby stream to speed the oxidation process so that it would match the aged siding. They preserved most of the floor plan and kept all of the original floorboards and doors on the ground level. Their contractor ripped out the insides of the exterior walls, adding insulation and finishing them with sheetrock that was then painted with a skim coat of plaster—Don's own recipe: rabbit-hide glue, slaked lime, pigment— for an impressively aged feel. "He was amazing at taking things apart and putting them back together so that we had a modern insulated house that looks old," says Don.

Inside, their home is peppered with pieces by Don (who embarked on a career as a furniture designer after twenty years in fashion), including more than a few love letters to Ray: A bed frame in a guest bedroom was made for Ray's previous apartment. When they moved it upstate and it proved to be too big to fit up the stairs, they cut it in half and then joined it back together. Hanging in place of a closet door is a quilt that Don made for Ray from fabric swatches—a testament to Don's ability to salvage seemingly unusable scraps such as the house's antique radiators, outlets, fixtures, sinks, and even toilets.

Preserving the quirky charm of the house was imperative. "Anything we could keep original, we did," says Ray. And their home teems with a stopped-in-time kind of magic.

In a reading nook, a collection of vintage aqua-glazed ceramics lines a shelf among the books. In the living room, overleaf, a well-loved couch and airy fern keep good company with Don's pieces, including a credenza with an intricate basket-weave design on its surface.

UPSTATE

Don designed the hutch in the kitchen and had a local cabinet-maker
build it from repurposed barn wood to look as if it had always been
there. The lower doors conceal a dishwasher.

"When I met Sohail he was already looking for a job outside of the city and I said, 'Okay, wherever you go, I'm gonna come with you,'" says Sara Zandi. "We had been dating for three weeks."

Main Street Bovina comes in just short of a mile. By the time you enter town, you're already leaving. Mostly residential, the street is punctuated by a general store, a church, and a second place of worship: Brushland Eating House, the Zandis' restaurant. When the couple found their way to Delaware County in 2014, their timing was propitious. There was nothing in the town, or even the immediate area, that ticked the specific culinary box—simple New American food made with ingredients sourced from area farms—that Brushland now does. You can't talk about Sara and Sohail's house without first considering their restaurant. From their kitchen sink you have but to look out the window to see it standing there, big but charming, right across the street.

For their first five years in Bovina, Brushland was the Zandis' kitchen (and their living room, their dining room, their bar); the house was where they went

BOVINA

1890

to sleep. "It was like camping," says Sara as Lou, a black stallion of a Great Dane, and Frankie, a caramel pull of a Chihuahua, wander in together, a dependable comedy duo. Sitting now in their home—a jewel box with soft plastered walls, natural light, and tall paned windows looking onto a lush expanse of green cut through by a rushing stream—it's hard to imagine it as anything else.

But when they bought the house in 2015, it came with a formidable list of challenges, including a makeshift kitchen (almost one tent short of a campsite) consisting of a plywood table, a sink, and an electric oven that they were too scared to plug in. The upstairs bathroom was "terrifying"—the ceiling and all the walls were missing drywall, which left the insulation spilling out from the skeletal framework. But running a restaurant and several guest houses took up the Zandis' bandwidth and it wasn't until spring 2019 that the couple could really roll up their

sleeves. "It only took us four years to finish three rooms," laughs Sohail.

They began by relocating their front door, which originally opened out to the street, to the back of the house for privacy. Sohail sanded the jaundiced pine floors, then finished them with five coats of lye, rubbing out all the yellow, while Sara went to work sanding and painting the kitchen cabinets ("I'm the paint lady, I'm not the floor lady"). And although their new kitchen is what domestic dreams are made of, they have yet to cook a single thing in it. "It seems less practical," says Sohail. Old habits die hard.

The couple's biggest coup was scoring a 1970s Percival Lafer sofa and chair set off eBay thanks to Sohail's talent for thrifting.

UPSTATE

Fog settles over the woods beyond Bovina.

To say that James Coviello has a thing for antiques is an understatement (or as he puts it, "I collect an-tiques, obviously.") His 180-year-old Greek Revival bristles with them. James—design director at Anna Sui—bought his first antique, a nineteenth-century brass picture frame with ornate foliate ornaments, when he was only thirteen. "I've never seen anything like it since," he says.

James moved into his Craryville house twenty years ago with just a mattress and some lamps, but to walk through it today is to experience an unfolding series of thoughtfully composed vignettes, all layered with precise artistic purpose. Postcards and scraps of paper are tucked into picture frames, antique mag-ic lantern glass slides from a Paris flea market stand propped on windowsills, and lines drawn on a pantry doorframe mark the heights of guests. On the upstairs landing, which James treats as another room, are dis-played a collection of mounted antlers and two very colorful Fair Isle sweaters, his "gardening drag."

Creating beautiful things is James's obsession. "With fashion, 99 percent is not creative, it's business.

CRARYVILLE

1840

I've been able to be purely creative with this house—it's been my art project for years." Curatorial eye aside, his most compelling collections have been shaped by his personal relationships. The flock of cuckoo clocks—twenty dollars for a box full—in the guest room are an ode to his mother. "My mom is from Switzerland and she's the only one in her family who ever left. I think it has a lot to do with how this place looks; her aesthetic sensibilities come from a different place, culturally."

James's collections are also what make the house his home. "For many years it didn't feel cozy . . . It just didn't feel personal," he says. So he grew his collections, and like the objects themselves, the stories behind them abound. A crowd of lusterware atop James's bedroom dresser came to him as if through a modern-day *Gift of the Magi*. A former boyfriend, who lives in Savannah, had a weakness for nineteenth-century lusterware; James has a fondness for nineteenth-century Old Paris porcelain.

"I'd been picking up lusterware pieces for him here in New York, and he'd been collecting Old Paris vases for me in Savannah, and then neither of us was willing to give up the collections we bought for each other," he laughs. "So now we each have a collection of both."

Downstairs, a group of little pinched ceramic houses takes up much of a small table in the sitting room—the unified effort of many hands captures the spirit of his home. "I had this epiphany that when friends come over for drinks, I'd give them some sort of artistic activity. I had this big lump of clay and I said, 'Just make a building,' and now I have a village."

James's collections of Victoriana decorate every surface.
While working on the house, he removed a layer of flooring
and was thrilled to find the original wide boards underneath.

James's love of cooking and penchant for collecting informed the design of the kitchen: the sink here is reserved for washing heavy pots and pans, while another sink in a narrow butler's pantry is used strictly for his collection of delicate antique glasses and porcelain dishes.

James's tiger maple Jenny Lind bed (circa 1850) was one of the first things bought for the house. Vintage striped fabric from a flea market hangs from a nineteenth-century French baldachin that he found on London's Portobello Road.

It's not hyperbolic to say that Kelli Cain and Brian Crabtree have seen most of the United States; their peripatetic and unconventional lifestyle is a happy by-product of their careers as musicians and their joint project, softbits, a sometimes-improvisational mix of electronic and experimental "really weird stuff" that has led them across the country.

DELHI

1820

It might be just as fair to say that their search for a home was an exercise in improvisation. Their house in Delhi was found, circuitously, thanks to a trip out west: the couple had explored the idea of buying in California and were visiting Brian's family there when they ran into a friend based in Hamden, New York, who tipped them off to the pleasures of life upstate. Kelli and Brian abandoned their hunt in Los Angeles and turned their gaze to the Catskills.

In Delhi they found two abutting century-old farmhouses, each a warren of low-ceilinged small rooms, with a floor that sagged where the two build-ings were connected. The couple combined the two houses to make a single 1,400-square-foot space that would also include a studio for Kelli, a self-taught

ceramist. Equipped with the technical skills that art school tends to foster, Kelli and Brian tackled their home renovations with the optimism and abandon of people who had never taken on a project of such scope. "There were no stairs for a while, just a ladder to the second floor," laughs Kelli. Brian eventually built both staircases, and when the couple found that their cement floors had been poured imperfectly, they ground them down with just one hand-grinder between them, creating "an inadvertent terrazzo effect."

Though the house underwent a gut-renovation, evidence of its past life is everywhere. The massive sliding door that separates the living space from Kelli's studio was made from the original floorboards, the dining table is fashioned out of repurposed wood joists, Kelli's studio work table was made using reclaimed wood found around the property, and a lone post that was moved to support the weight of the stairs is original to the old house.

Windows that wrap around the dining nook offer a view of the gardens where Kelli and Brian have planted an impressive miscellany of items: fava beans, garlic, onions, shallots, potatoes, peas, beans, tomatoes, tomatillos, jalapeños (the couple makes a mean fermented jalapeño sauce), daikon, Chinese cabbage (for their healthy kimchi habit), brussels sprouts, cauliflower, kale, chard, and collards. Just past the abundant gardens—and the couple's tour van—stands an enormous barn, where Kelli and Brian lived for five months while they renovated the house. It appears, a towering secret, at the end of their long dirt driveway, the connecting service road having been swallowed up by thirty-five acres of lush green-on-green that includes wild blueberries and a grove of apple trees the couple planted—just some of the more than 160 trees they've added to the property in their eleven years there.

The barn now houses the office for Monome (Brian's electronic instrument business), an extension of Kelli's studio, and a space for the occasional music performance and dance party. It's easy to imagine music mingling with the hum of crickets, bouncing off the crowds of trees that surround the barn, and rushing through their rustling leaves.

Kelli and Brian converted a three-sided fireplace into a pizza oven; the front hearthstone is made from the house's original doorstep.

UPSTATE

Kelli and Brian made the dining table from repurposed wood
joists salvaged during renovation. Kelli's handmade ceramics line
the shelves of the adjacent kitchen.

Among stacked sugar maple logs, the couple grows shiitake, oyster, lion's mane, and wine cap mushrooms.

Architect Mimi Madigan bought the plainspoken upright piano in her front room for looks alone. "It's from Amsterdam and, from what I'm told by our very earnest piano tuner, it has a satisfactory sound and is suitable for the kids to learn on. But no one is becoming a concert pianist on this piano," she laughs. This little fact serves as a direct contradiction of Mimi's architectural pragmatism, demonstrating that she too can be seduced by aimless beauty.

ANCRAM

1840

It's a summer Saturday and cross breezes rush through the windows of her perfectly symmetrical house. Her six-year-old son is doing the worm on the floor and Mimi asks him to maybe try that outside or, better yet, go on the zip line—a zip line that's part of a play structure that she built. "I spent the first two weeks here thinking, If I don't create something outside, I'm going to go crazy," she says. Which led to the outdoor shower. And the stone patio. And then the mudroom at the bottom of their cellar door entry. "It has transformed our lives. Everyone—dog included—can come in filthy and walk up into the house clean," she laughs.

When it comes to work around the property, Mimi's architectural training puts her in the driver's seat, where she's quite comfortable. "This house is my project," she says, and laughs, "At least one person in the relationship has got to be handy. That's vital for an upstate house."

Her husband, Greg, an attorney, is running late. He missed his train up from the city and by the time he arrives home, the couple's sons and dog—Pretty Boy Floyd, a Spinone Italiano—are beyond thrilled to see him, all three orbiting him in synchronized gambol, electrified by the idea of running wild outdoors. For the boys—and Floyd—being inside means carefully navigating a perfectly composed minimalist landscape that's both intentional and a continuous work in progress. It's upstairs in the attic, the boys' bedroom and playroom, that they have free rein to bump into whatever they please. "I don't want to always be yelling 'No' at them—I do enough of that downstairs.

Up there I just want to say, 'Do whatever you want,'" says Mimi, who knows when to pick her battles.

And she admits that there was a stretch when maintaining the house felt like an uphill climb. "There was always a project, or something would be going wrong. We were still struggling financially; we had the rent in the city and our mortgage up here. I just always had a worry about it—we'd come down this ridge and I'd get this knot in the pit of my stomach, like a tree had fallen on the house or there's a dead skunk in the attic, and it was dread, like I was in over my head."

But they made it through. "Two years ago, that's when I felt like I had my nice things, I had my people, we have nice neighbors . . . Okay, this is a house and it's our house and it's a keeper."

UPSTATE

Mimi and Greg's home is all open, airy spaces punctuated by pops
of color and precisely placed clean-lined midcentury furnishings.

A minimalist but warm bedroom offers space to relax and a sunny,
peaceful corner to read.

UPSTATE

You could say that a talent for interior design runs in Amy Ilias's family—her parents' New York City apartment was featured in the *New York Times* when she was a child. The handsome midcentury wall unit that Amy inherited from them now serves as the focal point in her front sitting room. "Their apartment was so spectacular. It had ribbon dividers and it was like a time capsule. I basically grew up in Don Draper's bachelor pad," she says.

HUDSON

c. 1825

Where Amy's parents' apartment existed as an ode to all things midcentury, the Lavender Ghost (Amy and her husband Jim Denney's moniker for their pastel-painted home) pulls heavily from Amy's travels during her tenure as art director at ABC Carpet & Home. Her first job out of college was working for a bookbinder in Soho who shared a space with a lacquer company. "The fumes were insane. It was like a toxic wasteland," laughs Amy. "And it was freezing in there—we wore insulated silver suits and fingerless gloves while we sewed the books." The story came to mind as Amy showed off the oddities and mementos displayed in a velvet-lined Victorian cabinet—bowls

from Vietnam, antique enameled pieces, old snuff boxes—each recalling lacquer-ware. These collections of alluring collateral jostle for attention in the many corners of the Hudson home. A glass cabinet in the dining room presents one such crowd, though the live edge wood table nearby steals the show.

The table was one of the first things Jim made for Amy, and he carved their initials into its side. It's common enough for college students in the northwest to take a summer job as a wildland fire-fighter, as Jim did while studying in Or-egon, and the experience instilled in him an abiding connection to and profound respect for nature, which inform his art—both his furniture and his abstract landscape paintings.

Living in a two hundred-year-old purple-hued Victorian was not the plan. "We always said, 'Anything but an old fucking Victorian house,' but it's funny because we both walked in and we were like, 'THIS IS THE HOUSE.'" Ending up together was also unanticipated, at least to them—Jim had been Amy's painting teacher at Carnegie Mellon, and, after running into each other a while later, he invited her back to the university to give a talk. "Nobody was surprised except for the two of us," says Amy.

Naturally Jim and Amy brought their artistic sensibilities to the renovation of their home. "This was our art for two years," says Jim. "This house is our little art project—our 'little' six thousand-square-foot art project." Artistic en-hancements aside, Jim views their roles as homeowners as beautifully imper-manent. "This isn't our house," he says. "We're just stewards. Someday we'll be gone, and this place will belong to some-one else. We're just taking care of it in the meantime."

"I knew I wanted something like this in here from the minute we first saw the house," says Amy. "Jim built the base, and the cushions are custom made. I love a good nook."

Amy purchased the ornate bed frame in India during a buying trip for
ABC Carpet & Home, and the workshop at ABC stripped the finish
and extended the frame to fit a full mattress.

"The basement is always a surprise," says Dan Lat-
insky. "There may be a video floating around of me
wrangling a small snake from under our washing ma-
chine while screaming." Sarah Elliott, the photographer who shot the homes for the book you're holding
in your hands, and Dan, her husband, didn't realize
just how intimate they'd be getting with four-legged
(and no-legged) creatures when they moved into their
1790s Greek Revival farmhouse. There was a pregnant woodchuck–"A very noisy roommate"–that nest-
ed under their porch one spring, and an infestation
of powder-post beetles that made quick work of their
entire sunroom floor.

HILLSDALE

c. 1790
& 1820

   Adding to these facts, the interior of the house
was in need of a coat of lead paint encapsulant, followed by a coat–or two–of white paint. "So, all in all,
we painted the entire 3,500-square-foot house four
times. It was a mission," says Sarah. As if that weren't
enough, they followed it up by personally tackling the
restoration of all of their windows: twenty-two in five
months, the second leg of their remediation journey.

This sort of focused determination is at the center of so much of their home. Take for instance Dan's artful Norweigan wood stack in the front of the house. ("Our neighbors are like 'Whaaaat?!?' We got a lot of slow drive-bys and a couple complete stops in the middle of the road.") Or the safari chairs that Sarah bought at a Paris flea market that now anchor the living room, looking very much at home by the fireplace. "They fully break down so I disassembled them and packed them in my checked bags."

Evidence of the couple's frequent travels (and Sarah's sharp photographer's eye) abounds. "My parents instilled the importance of travel in my sister and me at a young age; they'd always bring something home from their trips," says Sarah. "I chuckle when I see some of the ceramics we've MacGyvered into suitcases," laughs Dan, recounting the logistics of hauling some finds back from Oaxaca. "We spent our last night creating a bomb-proof suitcase to get the black vase that now lives in our living room and a large cooking comal home. After hours of arguing we managed to get everything to fit. We zipped up the suitcase and instantly heard the comal crack in half." The ceramics that did make it have been carefully arranged into precise com-positions by Sarah's thoughtful hand throughout the home.

The couple and all their treasures found their way to Hillsdale—a small town equidistant from Hudson and Great Barrington—after two nightmar-ish inspections on two different houses, one with a buried oil tank and no septic and the other with a failing roof. Considering their first two attempts, the state in which they found their current home was a boon for Sarah and Dan. After remediation, their biggest challenge was getting their gardening legs. "Last year was the first time both Dan and I have ever gardened in our entire lives," says Sarah. "We used grow lights to get a jump on the season and planted tomatoes, sugar snap peas, lettuce, red sorrel, some herbs, strawberries, and nasturtiums." As it turned out, the organic soil they bought for the garden was too rich in fertilizer and killed a lot of their seedlings. "We rallied, bought some more soil, mixed the two, and planted more," says Sarah.

An apt metaphor for first-time home-ownership, especially upstate where city transplants can find it challenging to make it in their new environment. Some wilt, and some bloom in the wild setting. Sarah and Dan have thrived.

On the shelves are pieces the couple collected on their travels: a worn teapot from Tibet, a dusty-hued vase from a mountain community in Oaxaca, and horn vessels bought in Kenya when Sarah lived there. On the mantel, a vase by Catskill-based Clam Lab was Sarah's first Mother's Day gift; she and Dan welcomed their son during the completion of this book.

Sculptural ceramic lamps by Kassandra Thatcher and side tables by
Black Creek Mercantile & Trading Co. flank the bed. A painting by Kate
Zimmerman Turpin hangs above. The master bathroom adopts the same
soft palette as the rest of the house, interpreted here in Calacatta Caldia
marble.

Acknowledgments

To the homeowners, for spending an eight-hour day with two people you had just met: you opened your homes to us, made us tea, fed us (from your gardens, no less), and inspired us, all while sharing intimate details of your lives. Thank you so much for your willingness to hop on that fast track to intimacy. I left each and every shoot bowled over by your warmth and kindness. Let's get dinner and drinks on the calendar ASAP.

To Sarah Elliott, for saying yes to riding shot-gun—despite actually doing all the driving—on this labor of love and shooting the homes while pregnant, like the true photojournalist you are. You are a fierce human with an uncompromising vision, an admirably keen eye, and a knack for fitting large ceramics and vintage safari chairs into suitcases. If MacGyver were a woman, he would be you.

To my agent, Carla Glasser, for finding me, pushing me, and advocating for me like crazy. I stand at least three inches taller with you in my corner. There's nothing more validating as a writer than being able to say "Email my agent," so thank you for that.

To my editor, Jenny Florence: working with you has been a case study in synchronicity. I have no proof that we ever finished each other's sentences, but for the sake of these acknowledgments, I'm going to say that it happened at least ten more times than it really did. I love that we value the same aspects of storytelling—the human touch, the simple truth, the small moments—and that we geek out on the same aesthetic details—the quiet ones that fly under the radar but that reveal everything about a home and a person. Thanks for fielding panicked emails, being generous with deadlines, and for knowing exactly what a writer needs to thrive.

To Monica Nelson, who designed this book, for framing my words and Sarah's photographs so beautifully. It's no small feat to bring disparate elements together and make them look like the classiest version of themselves. Thank you for wrapping it all up in the nicest paper and prettiest string.

To all my friends, for their endless patience and support and for being okay with me flaking out on a zillion plans because of this little project.

To my parents, for always believing in their children and supporting me no matter the endeavor. I've had the ridiculous fortune of being raised by two people who had zero preconceived notions of what I should be or do and who really, truly backed me in all my aspirations. Thank you for encouraging my sprawling imagination and creative disposition. I'm just sorry those art classes never paid off.

To my dad, for being my first editor and teaching me one of the most important tenets of good writing: say more with fewer words (see how I kept yours short and sweet?).

To my mom, who loves asking questions as much as I do and who, in the home stretch of the book, made herself laugh out loud every time (daily) she asked me, "Are you done with that book yet?" I have no idea what we're going to talk about now.

To William, for being my kid brother. Thanks for sitting in front of the computer in our parents' den spending hours writing ridiculous, ambitious stories with me. I'm so grateful that our imaginations and weird senses of humor mirrored each other so thoroughly. The snapshot I hold in my mind is this: two kids doubled over, holding their stomachs and laughing so hard at some stupid joke they'd written that they're crying. We were constantly thrilled at how clever we thought we were and I'm pretty sure we weren't wrong. You are missed.

To Zach, for being the pragmatic one. Eight years younger and somehow I feel like the little sister. Thank you for your support in this life, your genuine excitement about this book, and for giving us the "surprise dish" song.

To my husband, Jonathon, who drove my non-driver's-license-having-self all over upstate New York and for insisting I absolutely could when I insisted I couldn't. Thank you for finishing all the home projects I start, for splitting wood, cooking dinner, and always turning my side of the bed warmer on. You are the dictionary definition of "too good to be true."

—Lisa Przystup

Thank you to the homeowners who so warmly and generously welcomed two strangers into your most personal spaces. I immensely enjoyed photographing each of your homes, which are so uniquely YOU.

Thank you to my parents, Rob and Leslie, for always supporting my creative passions and for introducing me to and nurturing my love of travel and design from a young age. Thank you for teaching me to think outside the box and for helping to shape my photographic voice. You are two of the most selfless and generous people I know.

Thank you to Graham, Lauren, and Elliott for constantly inspiring me with your creativity and vision. Thank you for always lending me your eye to choose the best photo.

Thank you to my amazing husband, Dan, for wholeheartedly supporting this project and giving up so many precious summer weekends together. Your enthusiasm for wood stacking and your drive to tackle massive and overwhelming DIY house projects are just two of the many reasons I love you.

Thank you to my son, Jack, who was unknowingly present at every house shoot. I love you so much.

Thank you to Lisa, my partner in crime on this first-time endeavor, for bringing me onto this project and for trusting my eye and my driving. Your ability to speak to anyone and everyone as if you've been friends for decades is a true gift. Your warmth, positivity, and sense of humor made working together a dream.

Thank you to Jenny, our talented editor, for guiding us on the journey that was creating a book. From helping us choose the homes to selecting photos to reviewing proofs, your knowledge and expertise produced beautiful results that we could not have achieved alone.

—Sarah Elliott

Library of Congress Control Number: 2020934006
ISBN 978-1-58093-536-4

Printed in China

Design by Monica Nelson

The Monacelli Press
65 Bleecker Street
New York, NY 10012

www.monacellipress.com